BEWARE THE BURMESE PYTHONS

AND OTHER INVASIVE ANIMAL SPECIES

Written by Etta Kaner

Illustrated by Phil Nicholls

Kids Can Press

CONTENTS

SAVE OUR WETLANDS!

If you spot this invasive animal species, report it to your local Department of Fish and Wildlife!

Common names: nutria, coypu
Scientific name: *Myocastor coypus*

soft, dense underfur with long, coarse outer hairs

eyes can see underwater

rounded, ratlike tail

valves in nostrils and mouth close when underwater

large, sharp teeth

4 webbed toes on back feet

forelegs for digging out plant roots and burrows

Size

Body: 43–63 cm (17–25 in.) long

Tail: 25–41 cm (10–16 in.) long

Habitats

Near ponds, rivers, lakes and wetlands such as marshes and swamps

WARNING: ARMED (WITH TEETH) AND DESTRUCTIVE!

Invasion Route

INVASIVE

NATIVE

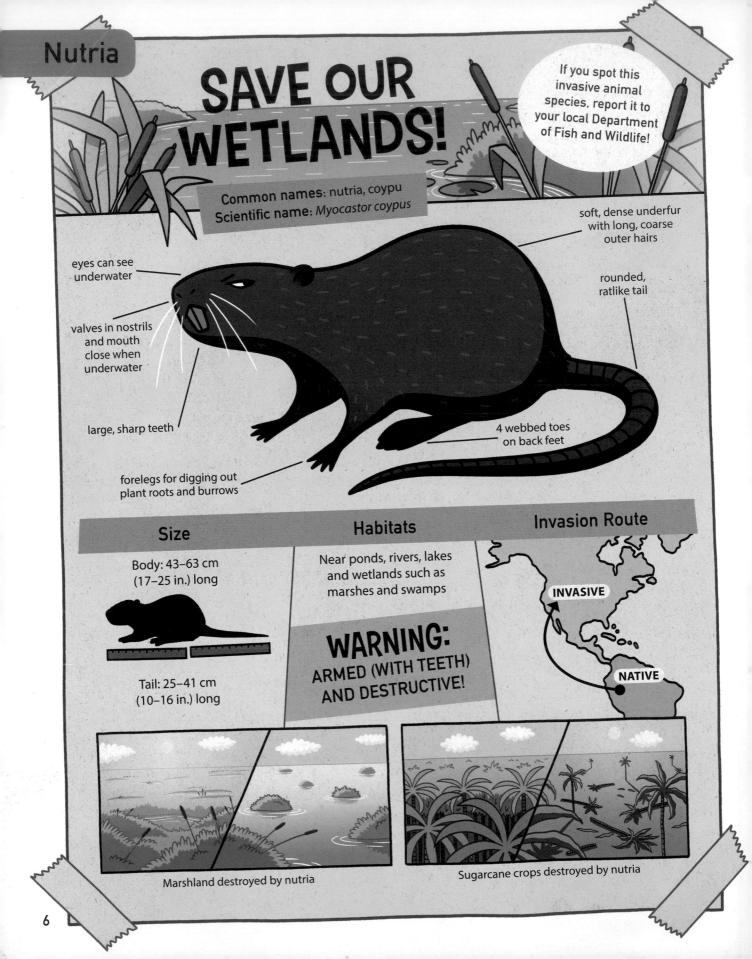

Marshland destroyed by nutria

Sugarcane crops destroyed by nutria

Invasion of the Veggie Bingers

When nutria were first brought to the United States from their native home in South America, no one thought they could be harmful. It was the 1880s and fur ranchers were planning to raise nutria to make fur coats. But after a while, fewer people were buying fur coats. So ranchers released thousands of nutria into the wild. Because nutria breed very quickly, it didn't take long for those thousands to become millions — millions with HUGE appetites. Nutria eat 25 percent of their body weight in food every day. That's like you eating 51 apples every day!

But hey, what could be so bad? Nutria are vegetarians, after all. The trouble is not only do they chomp on plant stems, they also love roots and rhizomes (underground plant stems). Eating these totally destroys the chance of a plant ever growing back or reproducing. And nutria aren't picky about their veggies, either …

These all look so nutria-itious. It's hard to choose.

NUTRIA MENU

Farmers' Crops
- rice
- sugarcane
- corn
- beets
- alfalfa
- wheat
- barley
- oats
- peanuts
- melons
- vegetables

Marshland Plants
- roots
- stems
- seedlings (young trees)
- leaves
- cattail rhizomes
- bulrush rhizomes
- cordgrass rhizomes

Side Orders
- tree bark
- rushes
- grass

AND THAT'S NOT ALL THE DAMAGE THEY DO …

What Can We Do about Nutria?

- Some chefs in Louisiana use nutria in their recipes to help save the local environment. The meat tastes like turkey.

- Marsh Dog, a company dedicated to saving Louisiana's wetlands, produces nutritious dog treats made from wild nutria meat.

- Governments are asking farmers to get rid of standing water in drainage ditches so nutria don't use them as homes or travel routes.

If you were a scientist or conservation officer, **WHAT WOULD YOU DO?**

HOP TO IT!

Be Part of the Solution!

If you spot this invasive animal species, report it to your local Department of Fish and Wildlife!

Common names: cane toad, giant neotropical toad, marine toad
Scientific name: *Rhinella marina*

hard, bony head

dry, warty skin

horizontal pupils

poison-producing gland behind each eardrum

slight webbing on hind feet

soft belly skin absorbs water

Size

10–15 cm
(4–6 in.) long

Habitats

Near fresh water in open forests, woodlands and grasslands

Invasion Route

INVASIVE

NATIVE

INVASIVE

WARNING:
POISONOUS AND ON THE MOVE!

Cane toad eggs

Cane toad tadpoles

Great Expectations

Did the toads eat the cane beetles? NO! What's worse ...

THE QUEENSLAND DAILY

CANE TOADS ARE TAKING OVER AUSTRALIA!

March 1: It's official. Cane toads have been declared Public Enemy #1 by the Australian Department of Fish and Wildlife.

According to biologist Benjamin Uness, these small creatures are a menace. "Cane toads are highly toxic," explained Dr. Uness. "Many animals that eat them are poisoned by toxins that ooze out of glands on their heads. This includes small dogs, snakes, lizards, birds, wildcats and crocodiles. Even cane toad eggs contain enough poison to kill fish and frogs."

Dr. Uness also explained that twice a year, "female cane toads lay up to 30 000 eggs at once, and the tadpoles hatch in about three days. In just one month, they become tiny toads, poisonous enough to kill small predators."

Dr. Uness went on to say that cane toads will eat almost anything they can swallow. Most of their food is insects, but they'll gladly munch on snails, birds, snakes and even small rodents.

To make matters worse, while cane toads lay their eggs in water, they are able to spend long periods of time on dry land. This means they can migrate easily. In addition, scientists say new generations of cane toads are moving at a faster rate because they've developed larger bodies and longer legs.

Dr. Uness warned that cane toads are a major threat to Australian ecosystems. They are poisoning native top predators. Fewer top predators means there are more herbivores eating plants. It's harder for smaller herbivores to find food.

According to Dr. Uness, much research is being done to find a solution to this serious problem. Let's hope scientists find one very soon!

What Can We Do about Cane Toads?

- Researchers use cat food to attract meat ants to ponds when young toads emerge. Meat ants love the toads' taste and aren't affected by their poisons.

- Some researchers are trying to train native Australian animals such as blue-tongued lizards to stop eating cane toads by feeding them bits of cane toad mixed with a chemical that makes them nauseous.

I don't feel so good.

- Scientists are capturing cane toads with traps that produce the same sounds that the toads make to attract mates.

CROAK

If you were a scientist or conservation officer, **WHAT WOULD YOU DO?**

DON'T BE A BIRDBRAIN!
Report This Pest!

If you spot this invasive animal species, report it to your local Department of Fish and Wildlife!

Common names: common starling, European starling
Scientific name: *Sturnus vulgaris*

mimics sounds of motors, music, human voices, other birds

strong bill muscles to find prey

reddish-brown legs

glossy green and purple feathers (white-spotted black in winter)

Size
About 21.75 cm (8.6 in.) tall

Habitats
Cities, open woodlands and fields

Invasion Route
INVASIVE

NATIVE

WARNING: Hangs out in MEGA-FLOCKS; can be VICIOUS!

Young starling

Tree with roosting starlings

Grape crop destroyed by starlings

Blame It on Shakespeare

Starlings Are NOT Darlings!

Cut to today. More than 200 million — that's the number of starlings that are now creating a crisis in North America! It's no wonder that wildlife departments are being bombarded by suggestions and complaints about these annoying pests.

Dear Department of Wildlife,

Who's the birdbrain responsible for all these starlings? They're devouring my blueberry, apple and cherry crops. They steal grain from my cattle and contaminate drinking water with their poop. My dog, Bingo, is hoarse from trying to chase these bothersome birds away. What are you doing about them?

Ms. Brown (farmer)

Hi there!

These starlings are bullies! I work hard to build a nest in a tree cavity, and they come along and kick me out. Even if my mate manages to lay eggs, starlings throw out our eggs or chicks and take over the nest. The same thing is happening to my bluebird, flicker and purple martin friends. It's not right!

Moody Woodpecker

What Can We Do about Starlings?

- Some farmers drape netting over grape vines and fruit trees to protect crops from starlings.

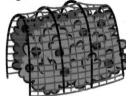

- Some American farmers sweep laser light beams across their ripe berry crops to scare away starlings.

- In Scotland, the Glasgow International Airport puts bird gel on its lights to stop starlings from roosting on them at night. To a starling, the gel looks like fire.

- Dutch inventor Nico Nijenhuis designed a robotic bird resembling a peregrine falcon. It's been used to stop starlings from destroying blueberry crops and to keep birds away from airports.

If you were a scientist or conservation officer, **WHAT WOULD YOU DO?**

DEPT OF WILDLIFE

Dear Department of Wildlife,

Starlings have chased away our native birds. But we can all make changes in our cities to encourage them to return. I suggest we plant trees in our yards and establish more woodland parks. We should also set up nest boxes with holes too small for starlings but just right for chickadees, swallows and bluebirds. Bring back our native birds!

Robin Jay
(environmentalist)

Dear Sir or Madam,

I'm an airline pilot constantly on the lookout for huge flocks of starlings, which can get sucked into my airplane's engines. This could cause major damage to the engine blades. And just think how it would affect the starlings! Please, please, please do something about them!

Peeved Pilot

Dear Department of Wildlife,

Our town needs your help. Our buildings, bridges, statues and vehicles are being corroded by huge amounts of starling poop. This is an emergency!

Mayor of Birdville

17

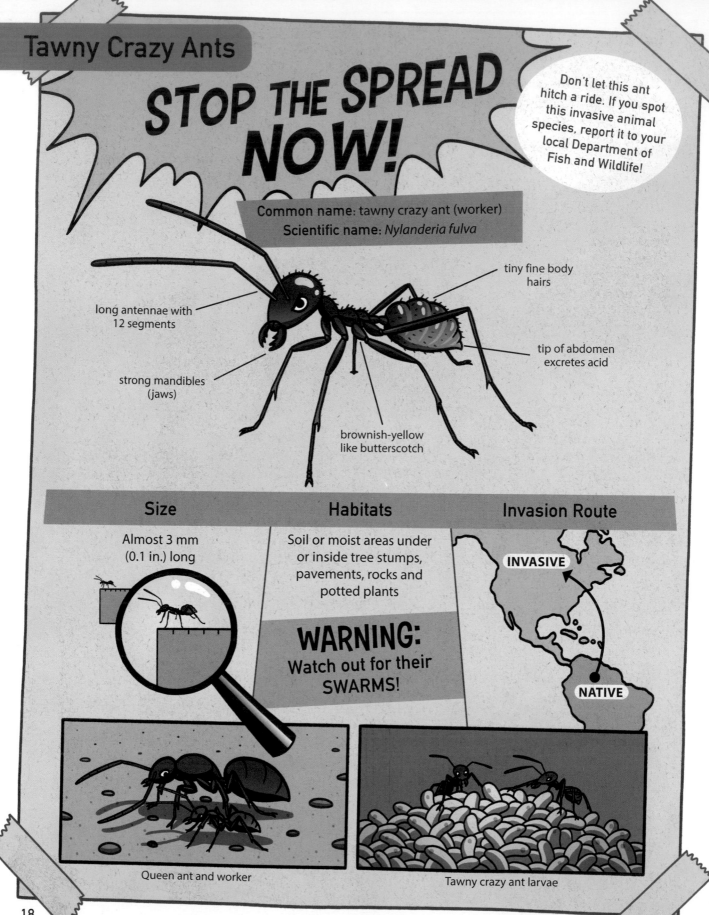

STOP THE SPREAD NOW!

Don't let this ant hitch a ride. If you spot this invasive animal species, report it to your local Department of Fish and Wildlife!

Common name: tawny crazy ant (worker)
Scientific name: *Nylanderia fulva*

tiny fine body hairs

long antennae with 12 segments

tip of abdomen excretes acid

strong mandibles (jaws)

brownish-yellow like butterscotch

Size

Almost 3 mm (0.1 in.) long

Habitats

Soil or moist areas under or inside tree stumps, pavements, rocks and potted plants

WARNING:
Watch out for their SWARMS!

Invasion Route

INVASIVE

NATIVE

Queen ant and worker

Tawny crazy ant larvae

Super Hitchhikers

Wonder how a tiny ant that doesn't fly could become an invasive species? By being a super hitchhiker. Tawny crazy ants aren't fussy about where they live, as long as it's warm, protected and has food. So when they get a chance, they hitch a ride and start a new nest wherever they end up. You may find tawny crazy ants hiding in …

Thousands of Ants, Millions and Billions and Zillions of Ants

The Texas Times
Crazy Ants Are Out to Get Us!

Homeowners are fighting a losing battle with tawny crazy ants. They're everywhere — in our walls and basements and even our cell phones. We can't get away from them, especially outside.

"My dog is terrified to go out to the yard," says homeowner Lianna Simone. "These ants just swarm all over him. And gardening is impossible!"

The Mississippi Star
Citizens Outraged by Outages!

Tawny crazy ants are causing dangerous power outages. Oddly enough, these ants are attracted to electrical equipment, such as air conditioners, phone lines, security systems, cars and computers. When the ants crowd inside a device, they stop the electrical contacts from connecting. This results in a power outage.

The Daily Gazette
Tawny Crazy Ants Harm Habitats

Tawny crazy ants breed so quickly that they outcompete every other kind of ant for food. This forces dozens of ant species helpful to our environment to move out of areas invaded by crazy ants.

As a result, native ants are no longer available to disperse seeds, help break down leaf litter and dead trees, and tunnel through soil, allowing air and rainwater to circulate. The loss of these ants is extremely harmful to habitats.

The Florida Sun
Ants Put Wildlife at Risk

"Thanks to tawny crazy ants, wildlife is seriously at risk," says environmentalist Candice Tenant. Massive numbers of them overcome and devour other insects, such as caterpillars, beetles, termites and wasps. This affects birds and other animals that depend on these insects for food. Very young, old or sick animals such as rabbits, possums and raccoons are also vulnerable. So many ants crawl into their eyes, ears and noses that they die of asphyxiation (inability to breathe).

The Louisiana Herald
Farmers Antsy about Crazy Ants

Farmers are worried about the damage tawny crazy ants can do to their crops. When aphids feed on the sap of certain plants, they produce a sugary liquid, called honeydew, that these ants love. So the ants herd the aphids to the right plants and protect them from predators. The more aphids, the better for the ants. But not for farmers. Aphids ruin crops by injecting plant leaves with toxins and diseases.

I can't help it if I have a sweet tooth.

What Can We Do about Tawny Crazy Ants?

- People should clear their yards of moist areas, piles of leaves and trash where tawny crazy ants like to nest.

- Farmers can get rid of aphids and other insects that produce sweet sap.

- Campers should check their equipment before leaving camping sites to make sure they don't bring unwanted guests home.

- People should inspect gardening supplies before moving them from one place to another.

If you were a scientist or conservation officer, **WHAT WOULD YOU DO?**

DON'T BE FOOLED!

This feral feline is NOT your typical house pet. Report this invasive animal species to your local Department of Fish and Wildlife!

Common name: feral cat
Scientific name: *Felis catus*

excellent day and night vision

ears that rotate for super hearing

long, sharp teeth

rough tongue covered with tiny hooks

muscular legs

razor-sharp claws

Size

40–60 cm (16–24 in.) long

Habitats

Deserts, forests, woodlands and grasslands

Invasion Route

INVASIVE
NATIVE
INVASIVE
INVASIVE

WARNING:
Feral cats KILL — even when they're not hungry!

Not picky about what they eat as long as it's meat

Small barbs on tongue

Tabby Takeover

In ancient Egypt, cats were the perfect pets. They were associated with several gods and were seen as sacred creatures that brought their owners good luck. Today, cats are still the favorites of many pet owners. But there are millions of feral cats (cats without a permanent indoor home) that threaten wildlife and disrupt ecosystems on every continent except Antarctica. How did this happen?

1500s to 1700s

Explorers and traders who sailed the world took cats with them to eat mice and rats that got into the ship's food supplies. Once the ships reached land, explorers and traders weren't the only ones to go ashore.

1700s

Cats were new to islands like Australia and Hawaii, and native wildlife had no natural defenses against them. One female cat and her offspring could produce 420 000 cats over seven years. It was just a matter of time before some native animals became endangered or extinct.

It didn't take long for feral cats to make their way to North and South America, Asia and Africa.

With their super hearing and eyesight, their sharp claws and teeth, plus their ability to stalk and pounce on their prey, cats are great hunters. Most wildlife doesn't stand a chance.

Plus, pet cats abandoned by their owners may become feral over time.

Cuddly Kitty or Cat-astrophe?

Many people, including scientists, are worried about the harm feral cats do to the environment and to humans. They think that governments should do something about it. But not everyone agrees.

Fish & Wildlife

Feral cats may spread deadly diseases like rabies and toxoplasmosis.

In the U.S., more wildlife is killed by cats than by cars, pesticides, window collisions and wind turbines combined.

Some Australian mammals are now extinct because of feral cats.

Cats are used as therapy animals. PURR-fect!

CATS ARE cute, clever and cuddly companions!

Biggest threats to birds: habitat destruction, climate change, collisions and pesticides. NOT CATS!

Feral cats kill 1 million reptiles each day in Australia!

Baby birds get less food and care from stressed parents when cats are nearby.

BIRD-KILLING CATS harm ecosystems! Birds pollinate plants, spread seeds, control insects.

Birds of prey kill birds too and no one makes a fuss about them!

We just do what comes naturally.

What Can We Do about Cats?

- It's illegal to abandon your pet cat or dog in Canada and most states in the U.S.

ADOPT ME

- Cat owners can put brightly colored collars on their pet cats to warn birds that they're nearby.

I look ridiculous!

- Volunteers in North America can participate in trap, neuter, release programs. They catch feral cats, take them to be neutered or spayed so they can't have kittens, and then release them.

- Veterinarians encourage cat owners to keep their pet cats indoors. (No outside trips for tabby!)

If you were a scientist or conservation officer, **WHAT WOULD YOU DO?**

Stop Invasion in Its Tracks.
DON'T THROW IT BACK!

Report this invasive animal species to your local Department of Fish and Wildlife!

Common names: rabbitfish, spinefoot, marbled spinefoot, dusky spinefoot
Scientific names: *Siganus rivulatus*, *Siganus luridus*

dusky spinefoot (*Siganus luridus*)

large eyes

marbled spinefoot (*Siganus rivulatus*)

small, rabbitlike mouth

spines on fins

Size

Up to 30 cm (1 ft.) long

Habitats

Shallow coastal waters near the sea floor, near coral reefs (native habitat) or rocky reefs (invaded habitat)

Invasion Route

INVASIVE

NATIVE

WARNING:
Spines are VENOMOUS!

Venomous spines extend when threatened

Skin has dark blotches at night or when threatened.

Shortcut to Disaster

When rabbitfish lived only in their native home, the Red Sea, they weren't a problem. But in 1869, the Suez Canal was built to connect the Red Sea with the Mediterranean Sea. Now humans no longer had to sail all the way around Africa to get to the Mediterranean. They could take the express lane through the Suez Canal.

What works for humans also works for fish. After several decades, rabbitfish figured out the shortcut. The southeastern Mediterranean had warmed up due to climate change and was a perfect environment for rabbitfish to multiply quickly. In fact, rabbitfish now outnumber all other herbivorous fish species in that area.

The rabbitfish loved munching on the algal forests (seaweed) growing on the Mediterranean Sea floor, and it didn't take long for those algal forests to become barrens (rocky bottoms without algae). As a result, hundreds of native fish species and invertebrates have been robbed of the algae they once used for food, shelter and nurseries for their young.

Scientists are also concerned about another invasive Mediterranean species, called foraminifera (forams for short). Their tiny shells, less than 1 mm (0.04 in.) long, have been piling up on rocky reefs by the millions, making it impossible for many native animals and plants to survive. Scientists couldn't figure out where the forams were coming from. But then …

1 Red Sea
2 Suez Canal
3 Mediterranean Sea

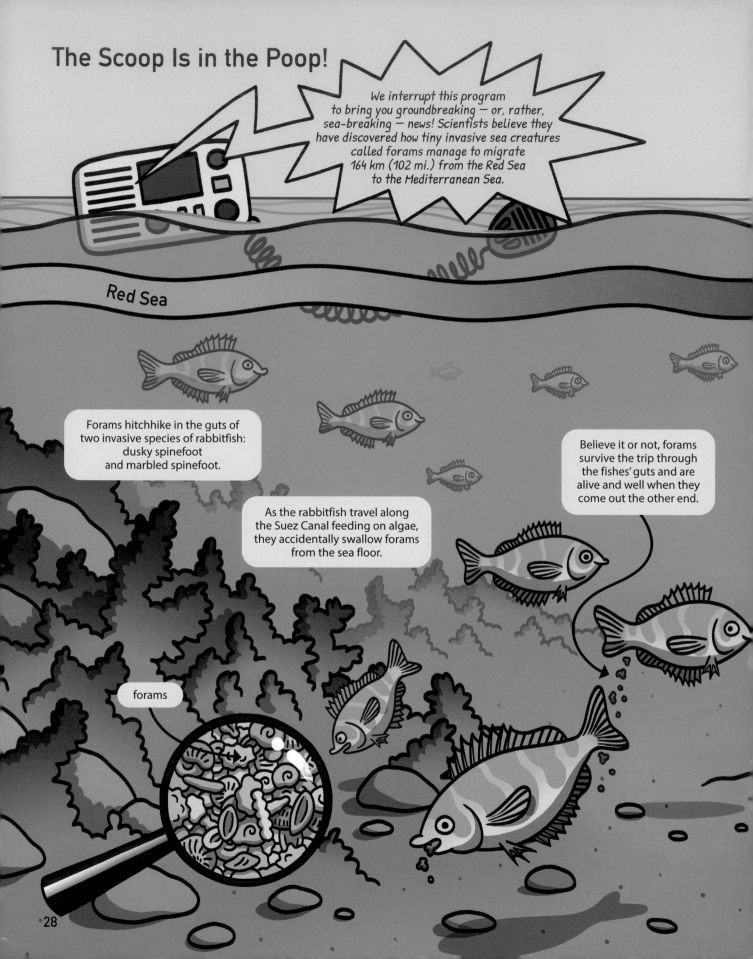

Mediterranean Sea

Over decades, the forams have also become an invasive species in the Mediterranean. Dead foram shells pile up on the hard sea bottom, turning it into a sandy surface where native plants and animals can't survive.

Scientists are concerned about the effect these two invasive species, rabbitfish and forams, are having on native species in the Mediterranean. They also worry that they will both move westward as climate change warms more of the Mediterranean Sea.

What Can We Do about Rabbitfish?

- Creating a rabbitfish fishing industry could reduce the number of rabbitfish that lay eggs.

- Serving rabbitfish in restaurants could lessen the amount of rabbitfish in the Mediterranean.

- Reducing carbon dioxide emissions could decrease global warming and the temperature in the Mediterranean, making it a less attractive habitat for rabbitfish. To reduce emissions, people can walk or bike instead of driving, plant a tree or a garden, start an eco-club at school … What ideas do you have?

If you were a scientist or conservation officer, **WHAT WOULD YOU DO?**

29

AQUATIC HITCHHIKERS!

STOP

If you spot this invasive animal species, report it to your local Department of Fish and Wildlife!

Common name: killer shrimp
Scientific name: *Dikerogammarus villosus*

curled, semi-transparent body

tail with two cone shapes topped with spines

2 pairs of antennae

3 pairs of swimming legs

large and powerful mandibles (jaws)

7 pairs of walking legs

Size

Up to 3 cm (1.2 in.) long

Habitats

The rocky bottom of slow-moving water in lakes, rivers and canals

Invasion Route

NATIVE

INVASIVE

WARNING: Can survive OUT OF WATER for several days!

Check your boat for hitchhikers.

Clean your boots thoroughly.

Clean and dry your nets.

How to Become an Invasive Species in Six Easy Steps
Learn from the expert — killer shrimp!

Step #1: Give yourself a cool name.

Killer shrimp earned their name by being vicious, often attacking creatures without eating them.

Step #2: Have lots of young.

Killer shrimp can lay up to 200 eggs at a time and keep laying them all year round. The shrimp can get so numerous that their natural enemies can't make a dent in their numbers.

Step #3: Be flexible about where you live.

Killer shrimp will live in fresh water or water that's brackish (a bit salty) and in water that ranges anywhere from 0°C to 35°C (32°F to 95°F). And as long as they're settled on a hard surface, they feel right at home.

Step #4: Don't be a picky eater.

Killer shrimp eat a wide variety of native wildlife, such as mayfly and dragonfly larvae, bugs, leeches, young crayfish, snails, shrimp (including their own species), damselflies, fish eggs and young fish.

Step #5: Be a clever hitchhiker.

Killer shrimp hitch rides in ballast (water pumped into the bottom of a ship to keep it balanced). At its destination, the ship dumps the ballast — along with its killer shrimp hitchhikers.

Step #6: Practice living out of water.

For up to six days, killer shrimp can easily hide among damp clusters of zebra mussels that cling to the sides of boats, or hang out in the folds of wet suits and nets, waiting to get to the next body of water.

If you follow these simple steps, you might become as infamous as killer shrimp. (If you want to be known as one of the most damaging invasive species in Western Europe, that is!)

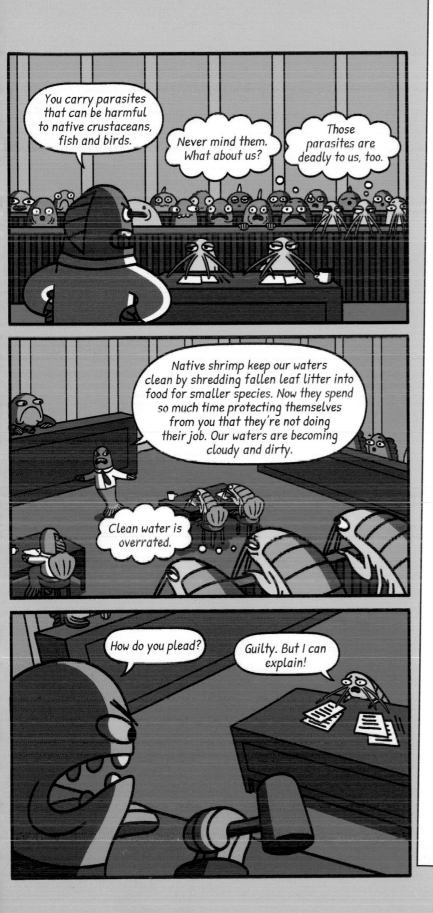

What Can We Do about Killer Shrimp?

- Boaters should check, clean, and dry their clothing and equipment after leaving a river or lake.

Hitchhiking is killer shrimp culture!

- At some sailing clubs, boaters can hose down their boats before entering a waterway.

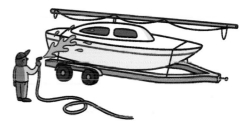

- Ships can use saltwater ballast, which killer shrimp can only tolerate for 24 hours.

Yuck!

- Scientists are researching ways to improve water quality so that native species can better compete with killer shrimp.

If you were a scientist or conservation officer, **WHAT WOULD YOU DO?**

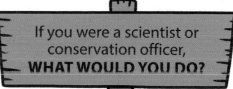

DON'T LET IT LOOSE!

If you spot this invasive animal species in the wild, report it to your local Department of Fish and Wildlife!

Common name: Burmese python
Scientific name: *Python molurus bivittatus*

6 rows of teeth
(4 on top and
2 on the bottom)

stretchy ligaments in
top and bottom jaws

heat sensors
in jaws

Size

Width: up to
35 cm (14 in.)

About as
wide as a
telephone
pole

Habitats

Marshy lowlands,
grasslands and jungles
near water

WARNING:
DANGEROUS! KEEP
AWAY!

Invasion Route

INVASIVE

NATIVE

They can reach the
length of 7 m (23 ft.),
about the length
of three beds.

From Popular Pet to Problem Pest

ALL MUSCLE!

Anything that crosses a Burmese python's path can be a meal — birds, mammals, even alligators. The python's flexible jaws allow it to eat prey three times the size of its mouth. In a lightning-fast grab, the python holds its prey with razor-sharp teeth while it coils its body around the animal. Then the python squeezes until the animal is dead before swallowing it whole.

After a large meal, a Burmese python might not need to eat for several weeks or even months.

But there may be tens of thousands of pythons in the Florida Everglades, all feasting on native animals! Scientists worry that many of these natives will become endangered or extinct either because their prey has been eaten — or they have.

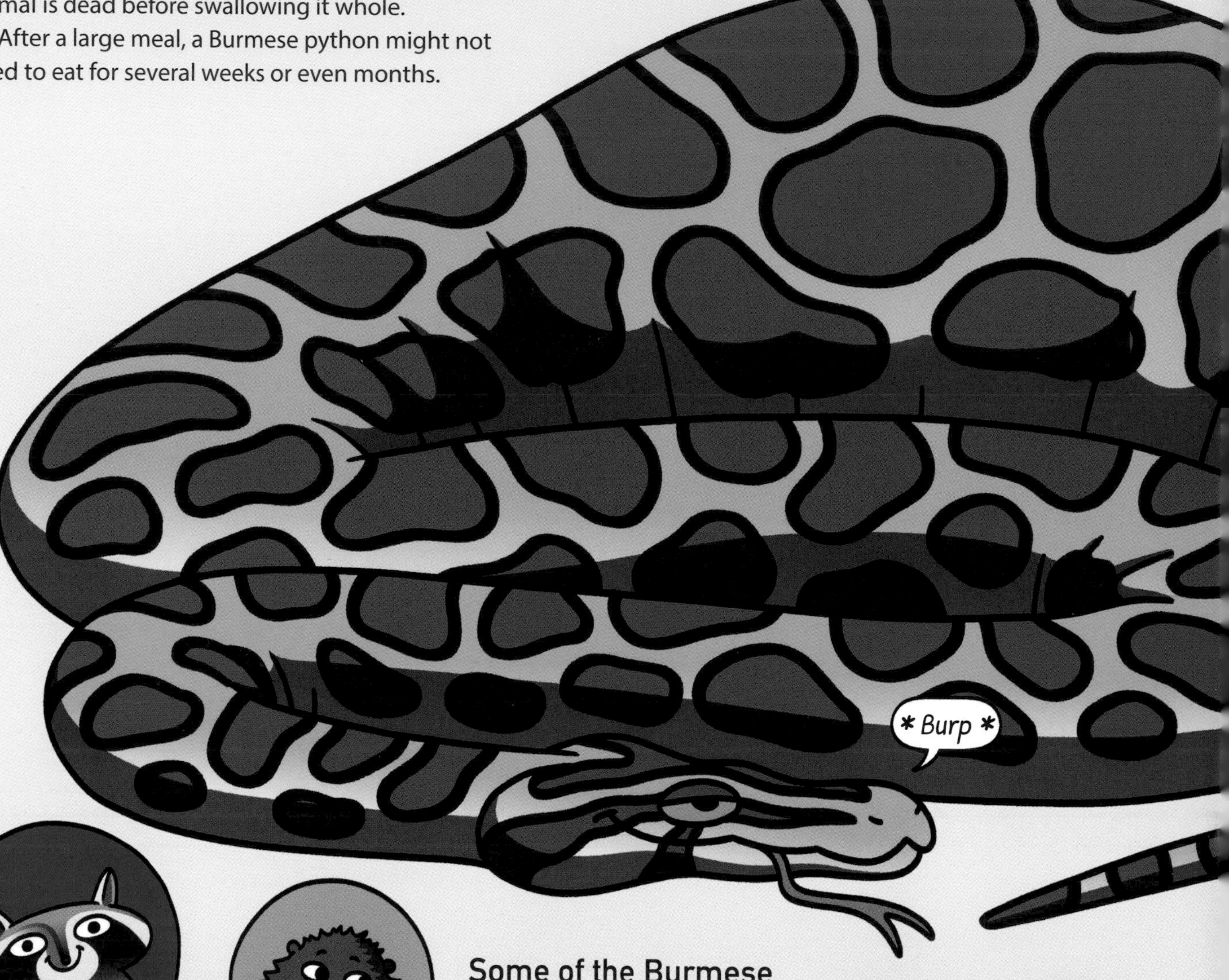

Burp

Some of the Burmese python's favorite foods

raccoon

muskrat

wood stork

gray squirrel

rabbit

deer

wren

What Can We Do about Burmese Pythons?

- Pet Burmese pythons should not be released into waterways.

- People need to learn how to identify a Burmese python so they can report it if they spot one. (Warning: don't get too close!)

- Researchers tag male pythons with radio transmitters to track them as they seek out breeding females.

- Florida holds a Burmese python–catching competition — with prizes! Adult participants must take a course before registering for the event.

If you were a scientist or conservation officer, **WHAT WOULD YOU DO?**

opossum

bobcat

mouse

small American alligator

Northern Snakehead Fish

If you spot this invasive animal species in the wild, report it to your local Department of Fish and Wildlife!

DO NOT THROW IT BACK!

Common name: northern snakehead
Scientific name: *Channa argus*

- long fins
- flat head with enlarged scales like a snake
- long, narrow body
- blunt tail
- large mouth with sharp teeth
- long fins
- blotchy, patterned skin with large scales

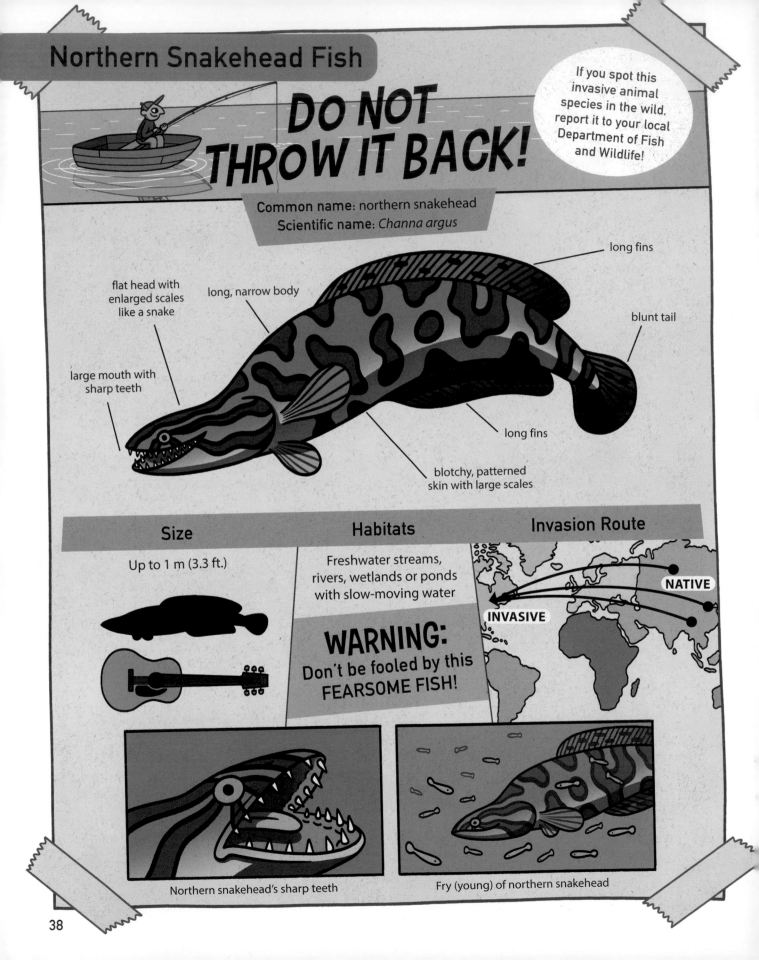

Size
Up to 1 m (3.3 ft.)

Habitats
Freshwater streams, rivers, wetlands or ponds with slow-moving water

Invasion Route
NATIVE
INVASIVE

WARNING:
Don't be fooled by this FEARSOME FISH!

Northern snakehead's sharp teeth

Fry (young) of northern snakehead

38

The Great Escapes

Northern snakehead were once popular as pets, as food in restaurants and in food stores where they were sold live. Unfortunately, things didn't always work out as expected.

The Perfect Movie Monster

It might surprise you to hear that snakehead have starred in four horror movies. Yes, four. That's because they have all it takes to become a harmful invasive animal species.

What animal species would make a good invader?

I know! Northern snakehead! They're ...

SUPER SURVIVORS

Northern snakehead easily adapt to new habitats. Low water temperatures? No problem. Temperatures as high as 30°C (86°F)? Sure. Ice-covered ponds? Fine. Low oxygen in the water? Easy! No matter what fresh water these snakeheads end up in, they thrive.

AGGRESSIVE

Northern snakehead devour almost anything, including fish that are one-third their body length! They also eat frogs, crayfish, beetles, small reptiles and even small birds and mammals.

POWERFUL PARENTS

These snakehead are aggressive when protecting their fry. Once a clutch of up to 50 000 eggs has hatched, parents circle around the fry in their special nest — a shallow column of water cleared of plants. They attack anything threatening. Protecting the fry for three to four weeks gives them a good chance of surviving.

TOP PREDATORS

Except for humans, adult northern snakehead have no predators. Nothing stops them from dominating an ecosystem. Fry and adult snakehead outcompete native species for food and shelter.

AIR BREATHERS

Northern snakehead have a lunglike organ that enables them to breathe air. That's how they can survive out of water in moist places for up to four days. Along with their ability to wriggle over land, they can easily take over habitats. How cool is that?

NEXT POND

That sounds perfect! I'm thinking four movies: Frankenfish, Snakehead Terror, Snakehead Swamp and Swarm of the Snakehead.

Four hit movies, coming right up!

What Can We Do about Northern Snakehead?

- Live snakehead should not be released into the environment.

- People who fish need to learn how to identify a northern snakehead so they don't throw it back if they catch one.

I'd rather be thrown back.

- It's against U.S. law to import live northern snakehead without a permit.

- By law, food stores in the U.S. can only sell dead snakehead to customers.

SNAKEHEAD $25

If you were a scientist or conservation officer, **WHAT WOULD YOU DO?**

41

Cactus Moths

BE ON THE LOOKOUT FOR THIS INVADER!

If you spot this invasive animal species in the wild, report it to your local Department of Fish and Wildlife!

Common name: cactus moth
Scientific name: *Cactoblastis cactorum*

grayish-brown upper wings with dark spots and wavy lines

long antennae

white or translucent hind wings

long legs

Size

Wingspan of moth: 22–40 mm (0.86–1.57 in.)

Larva (caterpillar) length: about 30 mm (1 in.)

Habitats

Sandy coastal areas, upland dry forests and humid forests

WARNING: Small but highly DESTRUCTIVE!

Cactus moth eggs in an eggstick

Invasion Route

INVASIVE

NATIVE

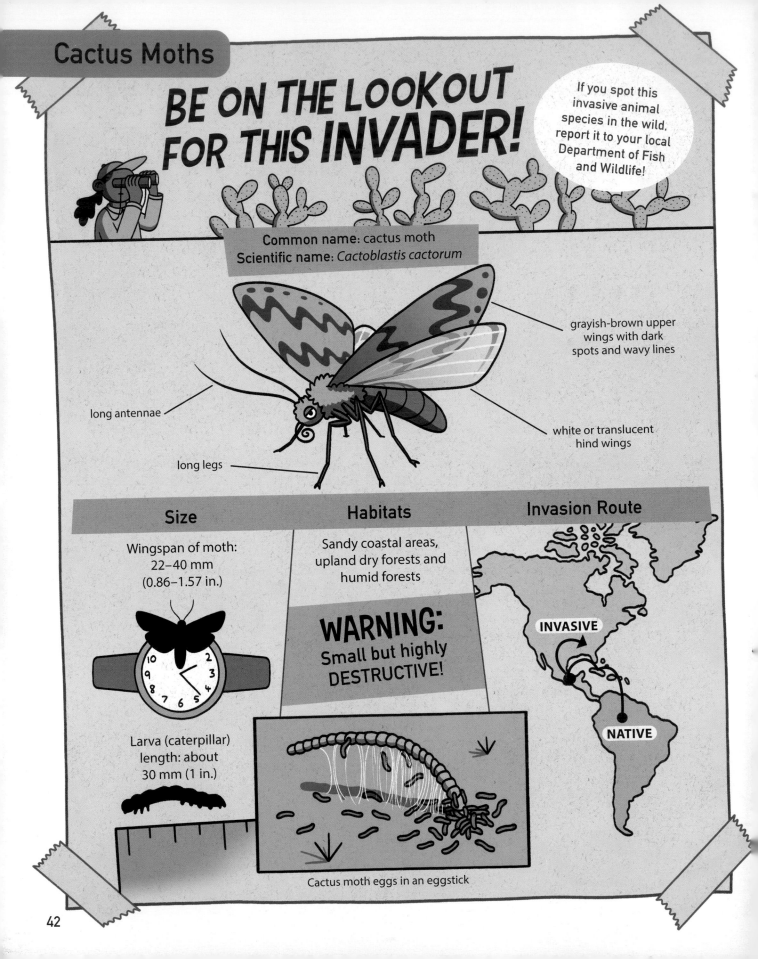

From Hero to Villain

Believe it or not, the cactus moth was once a hero. Australia imported these insects to prey on another invasive species — the prickly pear cactus. The moths were so successful that one town erected a monument to them, and other countries imported them to solve their prickly pear problems. Among these were several countries in the Caribbean Sea.

A few decades later, cactus moths showed up in Florida and Mexico. How did they get there? Some scientists think they hitched a ride when nurseries in North America imported cactus plants from the Caribbean. Others think the moths were blown in by storms. In any case, it didn't take long for the hero to turn into a villain.

It's not actually the cactus moth that's the problem. It's the larvae that hatch from its eggs. The female lays between 70 and 90 eggs in a stack, called an eggstick, on a spine of a prickly pear cactus. As soon as the larvae hatch, they burrow into the cactus's pad (flat stem) and chomp away, hollowing it out before they move on to the next one. In one season, a whole prickly pear plant can be completely destroyed. And that's just larvae from one tiny moth. Imagine what thousands of cactus moths can do to whole areas of prickly pears. The results are devastating.

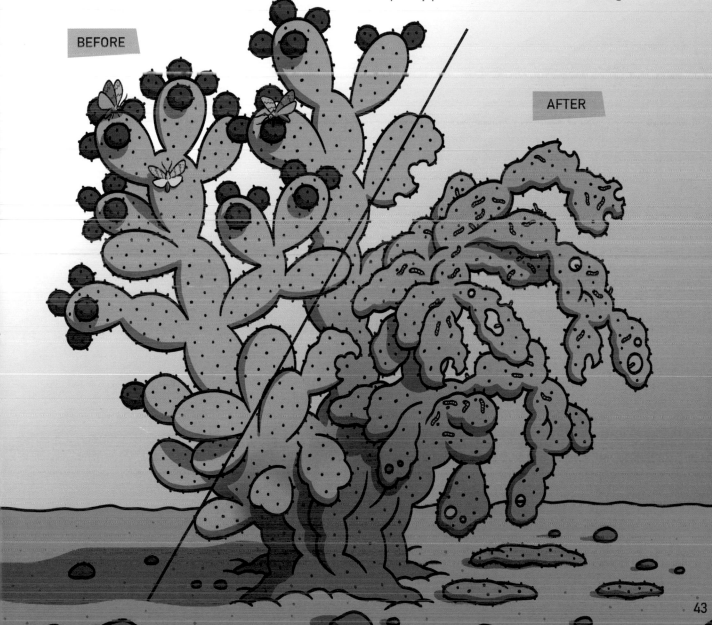

BEFORE

AFTER

Plenty of Enemies

In its native habitat of South America, the cactus moth has one main enemy — ants. This natural predator stops it from getting out of hand by eating its larvae. But in North America, though the cactus moth doesn't have any natural enemies, there are plenty of people who would love to get rid of it. Why? Because it's destroying the prickly pear cactus that so many, both human and animal, depend upon.

Some farmers make a living by selling prickly pear cactus pads and fruit to food stores, restaurants and manufacturers of food, cosmetics and medicine.

Many birds build nests in cactus stands. While the plants provide shade, fruit and seeds, the spines are also a great defense against predators.

Prickly pear cactus is an important water source for animals, such as the kangaroo mouse, pocket gopher and wood rat, that live in an arid (dry) habitat.

Bees, butterflies and many other insects drink nectar from the flowers, pollinating them at the same time.

Many Mexican restaurants use the pads and fruit in their dishes.

MENU

MAINS

Prickly pear eggs
Prickly pear tacos
Prickly pear chicken
Grilled prickly pear

SIDES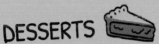

Prickly pear coleslaw
Prickly pear fries
Prickly pear salad
Veggie stir-fry

DESSERTS

Prickly pear sorbet
Prickly pear pie
Prickly pear cupcakes
Prickly pear cookies

DRINKS

Prickly pear smoothie
Prickly pear juice

Animals such as tortoises, iguanas, rabbits and deer munch on the juicy pads and sweet fruit. The fruit is also a tasty treat for beetles and birds.

What Can We Do about Cactus Moths?

- Ranchers are cutting down and clearing away infested cacti to stop the larvae from spreading.

- Plant nursery owners check plants for eggs and larvae.

- Volunteers are being trained to look for cactus moths and larvae in the wild and report them.

Hide-and-seek isn't fun.

- Government inspectors examine cacti that are imported into the country.

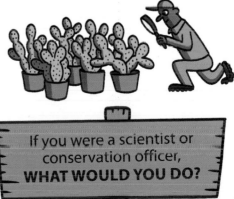

If you were a scientist or conservation officer, **WHAT WOULD YOU DO?**

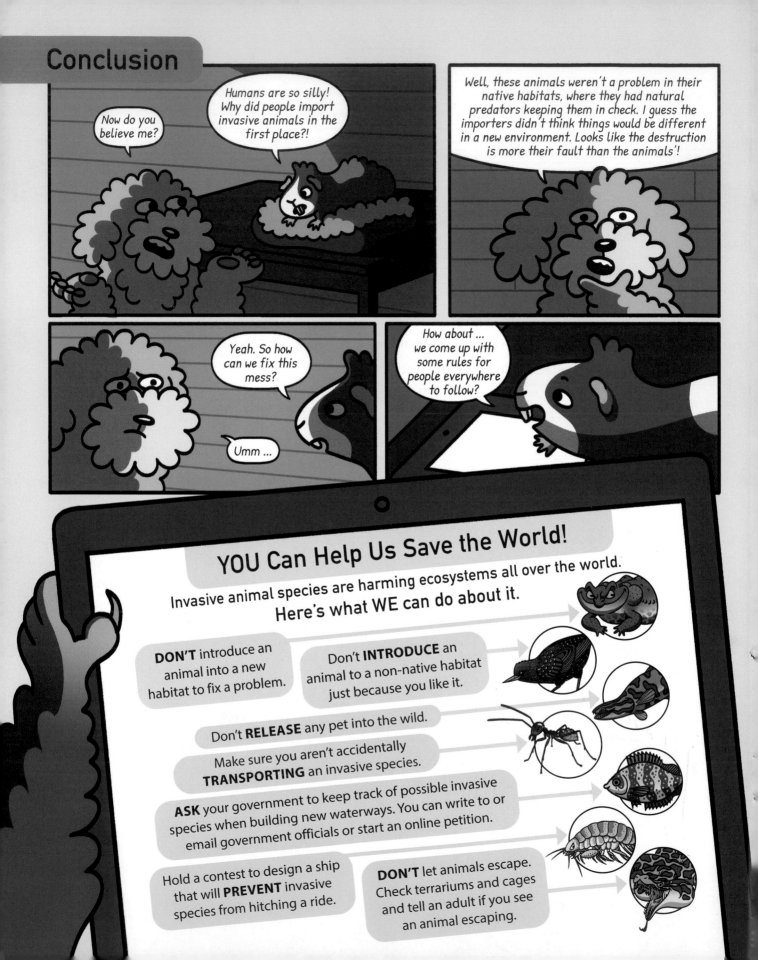

Glossary

alien: non-native, from another area

arid: dry, experiencing little or no rain

cavity: an empty space in a solid object

corrode: destroy or damage slowly

disperse: spread over a wide area

crustacean: an animal with a hard shell and several pairs of legs, which usually lives in water. Crabs, lobsters and shrimp are crustaceans.

ecosystem: a habitat in which the soil, plants and animals function interdependently with one another

emission: the giving off of something like gas into the air

endangered: when a species of plant or animal is at risk of going extinct

extinct: when a species of plant or animal no longer exists

feline: belonging to the cat family

herbivore: a plant-eating animal

infested: invaded by insects or animals in large numbers

invertebrate: an animal without a backbone

mandible: insect mouthparts used to grasp or crush food and to defend against predators

migrate: move from one region to another

murmuration: a large flock of starlings

nauseous: feeling like you want to vomit

neotropical: region including Central and South America, southern Mexico and the Caribbean

pollinate: to spread pollen from one flower to another

roosting: birds or bats gathering together in one place to sleep

sacred: used for a religious purpose

stand: a group of similar trees in a forest

toxic: poisonous

unstable: unsteady, fragile

venomous: poisonous

Selected Sources

Haupt, Lyanda Lynn. *Mozart's Starling*. New York: Little, Brown and Co., 2017.

Marra, Peter P., and Chris Santella. *Cat Wars: The Devastating Consequences of a Cuddly Killer*. Princeton, NJ: Princeton University Press, 2016.

May, Suellen. *Invasive Aquatic and Wetland Animals*. New York: Chelsea House, 2007.

May, Suellen. *Invasive Terrestrial Animals*. New York: Chelsea House, 2007.

Nagy, Kelsi, and Phillip David Johnson II, eds. *Trash Animals: How We Live with Nature's Filthy, Feral, Invasive, and Unwanted Species*. Minneapolis: University of Minnesota Press, 2013.

Shine, Rick. *Cane Toad Wars*. Oakland, CA: University of California Press, 2018.

Simberloff, Daniel. *Invasive Species: What Everyone Needs to Know*. Oxford: Oxford University Press, 2013.

Further Reading

Collard III, Sneed B. *Science Warriors: The Battle against Invasive Species*. Boston: Houghton Mifflin Books for Young Readers, 2008.

Kalman, Bobbie. *Invasive Animal Species*. New York: Crabtree Publishing Company, 2016

Metz, Lorijo. *What Can We Do About Invasive Species?* New York: PowerKids Press, 2010.

O'Connor, Karen. *The Threat of Invasive Species*. New York: Gareth Stevens Publishing, 2014.

For my darling David, an inspiration to us all — E.K.

To my parents, for always supporting me
and making me the nature lover I am today — P.N.

Acknowledgments:

A huge thank you to editor Kathleen Keenan for her attention to detail and creative thinking, to designer Barb Kelly for her incredible design and to Phil Nicholls for his laugh-out-loud clever illustrations. Thank you also to the many experts who reviewed parts of this book: Tamar Guy-Haim, Dr. Stephen Secor, Professor Rick Shine, Dr. Gary Witmer, Peter Stiling, Ed LeBrun and Norman Yan.

Published in Canada and the U.S. by Kids Can Press Ltd.
25 Dockside Drive, Toronto, ON M5A 0B5

Kids Can Press is a Corus Entertainment Inc. company
www.kidscanpress.com

The artwork in this book was rendered digitally.
The text is set in Myriad Pro.

Edited by Kathleen Keenan
Designed by Barb Kelly

Printed and bound in Malaysia in 3/2022
by Times Offset Malaysia

CM 22 0 9 8 7 6 5 4 3 2 1

FSC
www.fsc.org
MIX
Paper from responsible sources
FSC® C001507

Library and Archives Canada Cataloguing in Publication

Title: Beware the Burmese pythons and other invasive animal species / written by Etta Kaner ; illustrated by Phil Nicholls.
Names: Kaner, Etta, author. | Nicholls, Phil (Phil D.), illustrator.
Description: Includes bibliographical references and index.
Identifiers: Canadiana 20210348801 | ISBN 9781525304460 (hardcover)
Subjects: LCSH: Introduced animals — Juvenile literature.
Classification: LCC QL86 .K36 2022 | DDC j591.6/2 — dc23

Kids Can Press gratefully acknowledges that the land on which our office is located is the traditional territory of many nations, including the Mississaugas of the Credit, the Anishnabeg, the Chippewa, the Haudenosaunee and the Wendat peoples, and is now home to many diverse First Nations, Inuit and Métis peoples.

We thank the Government of Ontario, through Ontario Creates; the Ontario Arts Council; the Canada Council for the Arts; and the Government of Canada for supporting our publishing activity.